Cell Buddy

Story
by
Robert Johnson

Stage Adaptations
by
Ellen W. Kaplan
&
Jordyn Cahill and **Ellen W. Kaplan**

Art
by
Rachel Ternes

Cover design
by
Carla Mavaddat

Text design
by
Justin Song

A BleakHouse Publishing Reprint

2012

BleakHouse Publishing

NEC Box 67
New England College
Henniker, New Hampshire 03242
www.BleakHousePublishing.com

Robert Johnson – Editor & Publisher
Sonia Tabriz - Managing Editor
Liz Calka - Art Director

Shirin Karimi - Senior Creative Consultant
Erin George, Charles Huckelbury, Chris Miller, Susan Nagelsen,
& Saba Tabriz - Consulting Editors
Rachel Cupelo – Marketing Editor
Carla Mavaddat - Assistant Art Director & Curator

ISBN-13: 978-0-9837769-0-1

Printed in the United States of America

Table of Contents

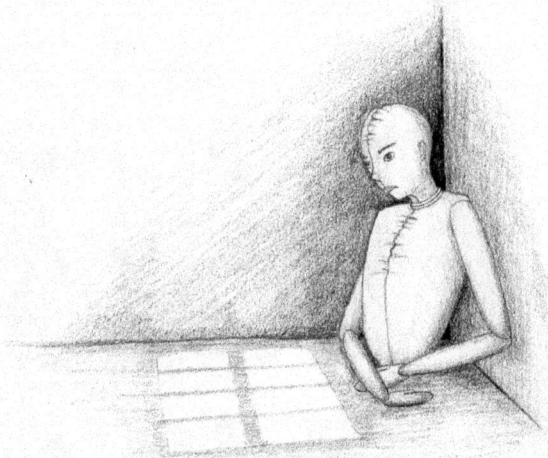

Cell Buddy
The Story

Robert Johnson

Amanda looked about anxiously, shifting her weight from one foot to the other as she stood in the commissary line. She'd noticed the big red box the day before but had hesitated. She didn't know a single convict who had one but she knew it was just what she needed. She was desperate. Anger was eating at her, her moods were turning sour, and her loneliness was taking on a life of its own. So here she was, placing her order.

"One Cell Buddy, please." She spoke in what she hoped was a calm, measured tone.

"Which model?" asked the inmate behind the counter, barely looking up.

"Which model?" Amanda asked, in a higher voice than she liked, sounding a bit girly. Amanda was thrown off balance for a moment. She didn't know Cell Buddies came in models and she didn't want to sound like a girl, though of course she was a girl, and in fact a girl once much sought after in the cellblocks. She paused. A small line was forming behind her.

"What do ya' mean, which model?" Amanda said, in a deeper voice, the one she cultivated for public exchanges in prison. "I want – I don't know, the standard goddamn model."

"OK, OK," said the inmate, raising her hands, palms up. "Just doing my job."

Amanda nodded.

"Black or white?" the inmate continued. "We're out of the mixed-race model."

Amanda paused, then frowned. Speaking carefully, "They make mixed-race Cell Buddies?"

"Brown. That's your standard Brown Cell Buddy. We do all the races. This is equal opportunity stuff."

After a pause, the counter woman said, snapping her fingers—and moving her hips—rhythmically, "You know, supply and demand, even in the can."

Amanda had begun to sweat. Evidently there were others in the House with Cell Buddies. There'd been a run on Brown Buddies, she thought. And what was the deal with this bitch behind the counter? She'd wanted this to be a hit-and-run thing but it was becoming a full-on conversation.

"White, for christsakes, white." Amanda was white, and she figured anybody in prison who crossed the color line on inflatable cellmates was looking for trouble.

"Papers?" The inmate now had her hands resting easily on the counter.

Amanda just stared at her, keeping herself under control.

"Adoption papers, hon." The inmate spoke as if adoption papers were an obvious consideration for a convict in the market for a Cell Buddy.

"They come with adoption papers," she continued, as if Amanda were a child. "You can fill in the name," snapping her fingers again, "and pop it in a frame."

"Frame?" A hint of nervousness had crept back into Amanda's voice. She considered turning on her heels and simply running back to her cell but was too embarrassed to move.

"We've got frames, all kinda frames. You're supposed to frame the papers. It's like a respect thing."

The woman behind the counter retrieved a big red box marked CB-White and handed it across to Amanda, together with a frame and adoption papers. Amanda gathered her haul, marked her signature on the commissary account line, then walked straight back the way she'd come. She was careful to keep the brightly colored package close to her body, hoping to avoid anyone she knew as she worked her way up the steps to her third-tier cell. When she got to the cell she looked both ways, then entered quickly, as if she were returning from a regular day at the prison canteen, eager to get her goodies put securely away, out of the view of thieves—women who moved in packs, grabbing sweets and treats and sometimes even TV sets and selling them on the black market.

But this was different, Amanda knew, really different. Snacks from the commissary were one thing; an inflatable Cell Buddy was decidedly another.

The woman at the commissary had been cool about it, like it was an order at a restaurant—but the give and take at the counter had put Amanda on edge. The whole business seemed sketchy. What did the girls in the line think about all this? Papers? Frames? Keeping one eye on the cell door, Amanda opened the box and

pulled out the folded plastic figure, gently removing the sealed packaging, complete with a two-part pump system she assembled after a few minutes of difficulty. (Amanda was pretty handy but sometimes struggled with instructions.) Now with her back to the tier, hiding the plastic figure from view, Amanda slowly pumped up her Cell Buddy until it was fully inflated. She then stood back, admiring her new friend.

Amanda couldn't help but think that her Cell Buddy cut a striking figure. A two-and-a-half foot torso, the Cell Buddy came standard with movable arms and a swivel head. The Cell Buddy was the brainchild of a psychiatrist who believed that convicts needed emotional support to help them get through their prison days. "Even convicts need love," she'd said. "Prison is a lonely place, especially for women." The arms were a special feature. "They are expressly made long," the psychiatrist had said, "long enough to wrap around the prisoner's body in a secure embrace."

Wardens and administrators affiliated with the prison system thought the Cell Buddy was a joke. They assumed all convicts crave sex, not love, and that a plastic figure with no orifices or appendages (Cell Buddies are smooth all over) would be a loser in the prison market. Amanda read this in a newsletter while she was waiting for her annual physical. "Easy for them to laugh," she'd thought, but the shrink was serious and for damn sure Amanda was serious. As far as Amanda was concerned, the psychiatrist was right on the money. Amanda was lonely, and she was frightened, and at times she was just plain mad at the world. There was no way to handle those emotions in prison without help.

That's where her Cell Buddy would come in, Amanda thought. Someone to listen; someone to make her cell a home.

Amanda knew that some of worst things that can happen to a woman in prison typically happened in her cell, at the hands of a cellmate she once loved, or thought she'd loved. Domestic abuse was a hidden epidemic in prison, Amanda knew from the echoes of grief reverberating up and down the tiers. "Who'd believe it?" she once told a visitor, early in her prison term, before she had any inkling of what lay ahead for her. "We don't have men here but we still got wife-beating!" The visitor looked at her like she was talking in riddles. Amanda dropped the subject.

Amanda had joked about getting a Cell Buddy for years, years she spent with her last convict cellmate, Danielle, aka Dan the Man or simply Dan. The butch girls often took male variants of their given names, to go with their big tattoos and bigger muscles, not to mention the cold stares they cultivated for their sojourns in the prison yard, where they'd shamelessly flaunt their male bona fides, walking slow and threatening, glaring out at the world, daring women to make their day. At first, Amanda loved Dan like a sister loves a tough, protective older brother. Nothing sexual; just sheer admiration. Dan made Amanda feel secure. Safety is an illusion in life, and especially in prison, but the fact is, Dan made Amanda feel safe. In prison, that is no small thing.

Back in the early days of their relationship, Dan often said, "Amanda, when I'm gone, get yourself a Cell Buddy. Don't leave the cell without it. Why be lonely when you can have a rubber homie." Dan was a bit of a homegrown poet, if you could be generous with your notion of poetry.

Dan was also, as it turned out, a bit of a predator. He was, in the words of the women on the cellblocks, a smooth operator— patient, willing to wait out his prey. Dan knew that Amanda needed him, knew she couldn't live on her own, knew she would be easy pickings for the other tough butch cons. Dan carefully cultivated Amanda's trust, then made his move. Dan the Man seduced Amanda with the classic prison line—it's either me, or everybody.

Amanda didn't see it coming, and in fairness to her, the process was subtle. You've got to give Dan credit; he knew what he was about. First there were requests for small favors (tidying Dan's part of the cell), then tentative requests for shows of support and affection, like a back rub after a hard day. "Hey, baby, that feels good, just like that, right." Then, gradually, Dan began giving orders—first for little things, maybe with an apologetic smile, things Amanda would have done anyway, like warming up his coffee. Soon Dan demanded anything and everything he desired. Like a kind of perverted Biblical patriarch, Dan the Man wanted dominion over Amanda in all things. He wanted sex (and on his terms), but even more he wanted her reduced to abject servitude. Dan wanted his bed made, he wanted his laundry done, he wanted his food served warm while he lay naked, looking at Amanda like she was a piece of meat. He wanted to use Amada as a punching bag on bad days, and there are a lot bad days in the Big House. When you come right down to it, Dan wanted Amanda to be his slave, his chattel to have and to hold and to abuse at will.

And Amanda was Dan's slave, meek and docile, pretty much right up until she killed him.

There were warning signs, but this time it was Dan who didn't see it coming. He didn't see Amanda's grief or her anguish or her rage, masked by an increasingly plastic, fixed smile. "Sure Dan, right away. Whatever you say." Always with the big smile, the too-big smile you might have found on an American slave plantation back in the day. Dan was no historian, and besides he thought of

Amanda as a slave, so he took Amanda's behavior in stride, as if it were his due. Dan definitely didn't notice the small rebellions or the furtive looks as Amanda prepared his bed for him at lights out. Amanda's lips would be pursed, her eyes ever so slightly narrowed in distaste, the bed never perfectly made, the coffee a tad bitter. Dan didn't catch any of this. And he didn't see the shank coming, the one Amanda plunged deep into his back while he slept.

Shank. Dan had been insistent about calling a homemade prison knife a shank. "It's a shank, Amanda, not a shiv. A shiv is gay." He'd walk the yard with Amanda and say, "See that bitch, the skank with the shank? Watch out for her." Shank, shiv, knife—whatever it was, it took residence in Dan's body, and Amanda was on her own, alone in the abusive home she'd shared with Dan, in the prison he'd made her personal hell.

**

The prison at night is a scary place. It's as if the cellblocks have a life of their own, populated by the haunted spirits of prisoners past. Amanda sensed these presences, thought she heard low, murmuring voices in the night, felt cool breezes brush against her skin. Somehow, beneath the cries and the rage and the ruin, Amanda sensed a deeper hurt, the hurt of pure loss, the hurt that tells you the one thing you never want to hear—that the world is hard and cold and you are alone, completely alone. There is you, and there is suffering, and there is loss.

At these moments, wrestling with a sense of dread, Amanda would clutch her Buddy close, glad for his companionship. Buddy, that's what she called him. Short and sweet, like the little man himself. Amanda needed to hold Buddy, needed the touch. The words of a poem she'd read kept running through her head. "O'er the cell a mark still lingers," it started, "Of where a convict's bloodied fingers..." As Amanda drifted off to sleep, the poem unfurled in her mind like a sail on a breezy spring day:

"Could make stone speak of life's hard ends
"With words that shine like darkling gems
"I was here
"I am a woman
"I bleed, therefore I am..."

8

Am what? For a moment, Amanda wasn't sure. Then it came to her: Alive.

> *"Alive, in a manner of speaking*
> *"It's raw, sweet freedom I'm desperately seeking*
> *"A prison cell's a coffin reeking*
> *"Of dreams gone sour*
> *"Of life died by the hour*
> *"Of death by decree*
> *"Until you're set free*
> *"In this life or the next."*

Amanda pulled Buddy closer, seeking warmth in his plastic embrace, hoping to shed the notion that her cell was in fact a tomb and that one day it wouldn't open and she'd be trapped there for eternity. "A prison cell's a coffin reeking…"

Trapped with Buddy. Well, that was something.

***

Amanda hated to let the air out of Buddy each morning but she couldn't take him outside the cell in his fully expanded condition. Prison has its strange byways—hell, she'd even read about a prison called Strangeways—but there are limits. Some of the cons looked and dressed like men, even attractive men, for heaven's sake, but toting a Cell Buddy crossed the line. People didn't seem to notice that Amanda had this folded plastic friend with her wherever she went, tucked under her arm. At least, no one said anything. Amanda wasn't sure, but she thought that perhaps the rest of the tier figured she'd lost it and might be dangerous. "Mess with Buddy," she'd said under her breath, as much a plea as a threat, "and you'll come up bloody." Some of Dan's poetry had evidently rubbed off on Amanda.

Still, Amanda thought she heard the sniggers and she imagined the insults. Boy Toy, that sort of thing. The other girls just didn't get it, Amanda figured, or didn't want to get it. A bunch of them had their own Cell Buddies, she knew, or else the commissary wouldn't carry them at all, let alone have different Buddies for each race. But these women evidently kept their plastic companions under wraps, afraid of what others might think. Now that she thought about it, she'd seen women with full, puffed out shirts now and again in the mess hall. Amanda had assumed they'd wrapped magazines and newspapers around their torsos, the prison's version of a shank-proof vest. Now she marveled at their ingenuity. Carrying their Buddies around in public, hidden in plain sight!

Amanda was less discrete because she didn't care. Prison was death; Buddy was life. You had to live, if you could. You didn't have to live well, but you had to live. That's just the way it is. Some people have to go to prison to learn that. Whatever else Amanda learned in prison, she learned she needed Buddy to live. So she carried Buddy out in the open, deflated, but right out there for anyone who cared to look.

At night, back in the cell, Amanda would prop Buddy up with a book in his hands, tilt Buddy's swivel head down slightly so Buddy could read, and carefully position Buddy in the middle of the bed, where he would be stable. Buddy had once taken a fall from the side of the bed, picking up a pretty bad scratch in the process when he hit the rough concrete floor. Amanda wasn't going to let that happen again.

"Feel all right, Buddy?" she'd ask solicitously.

Buddy would nod, or so it seemed to Amanda.

"Been a rough day, Bud?" Amanda would ask without much feeling. She was tired at the end of her prison day, if for no other reason than that she was protective of Buddy and worried that if some bad-ass bitch assaulted them, Buddy would be history. And if Buddy was history, Amanda would be history, too.

Buddy seemed oblivious.

Amanda, comforted by Buddy's silence, which she interpreted as his agreeable invitation for her to chat, would sometimes review the events of their day. "What'd you think of that Aryan 'ho, Bud? Me, I thought she'd lose it when you brushed up against her."

Buddy's head appeared to nod, however slightly.

"I mean, it's not like you're black or white. You're pure, Bud, almost translucent. You're your own race, know what I mean?"

Buddy shined in the glow of the overhead light, which had just then been turned on as the sun set outside the prison.

"I ain't no racist," Amanda continued, perhaps a bit defensively, "but I'm more comfortable with my own. That's just normal."

Amanda moved Buddy to the far side of the cell, just below the framed adoption papers, shielded from the view of passing convicts.

***

There were days that Amanda was all right and figured she was going to make it. Other days, she had her doubts. Some days, though, it seemed like she'd lost it for good. On the bad days, her temper had a life of its own. She thought her occasional explosions were normal, at least as normal as putting people in cages and leaving them to fend for themselves for years on end, sometimes with nothing more than a Cell Buddy for companionship.

Amanda had discovered a deep well of anger inside her after she'd killed Dan. She didn't even remember killing him, exactly, all she remembered was watching someone who looked a lot like her plunging the shank into Dan's back, over and over again, eyes wide, teeth bared. Like an animal.

And she had been an animal to Dan, a beast of burden. Dan was gone but the burden was still there, the burden of hurt and barely suppressed fury. Dan's abuse lived on, right inside her. The rank injustice of this made her blood boil.

At first, having Buddy cooled her hate, this toxic gift from Dan, but nothing good lasts for long in prison. Prison is like an inferno, Amanda thought, burning up everything good in a painful orgy of self-inflicted punishment. One night, the inferno raged out of control.

Amanda could make excuses for her episodes. Had Dan called his explosions episodes? Had she learned this from Dan?

He had a laundry list of excuses, when he bothered to make excuses, and now she did, too. She hadn't gotten a letter in ages. An old woman had stumbled and knocked the deflated Buddy from her arms, getting Buddy smeared in grease from the mess hall. That night, the cell lamp had burned out, so Amanda couldn't read and talk to Buddy on the schedule to which they'd become accustomed.

And somehow, Amanda couldn't really explain it, the smell of grease and the soft light of the cell at twilight, rays of a rising moon streaming through the bars of the cell window, had made Amanda amorous. She snuggled close to Buddy, drinking in his scent, redolent of fried food but appealing nonetheless, flushing and growing excited almost against her will.

"Buddy, Buddy," Amanda moaned, slowly letting go and liking it, moving easily to an inner rhythm as old as life itself but long denied to Amanda during her many years in confinement. Dan had raped her; that was violence, not sex. But this, she thought, this was something different, something good. Almost instinctively, Amanda rolled Buddy onto his back, looking at the little half-man through heavy-lidded eyes suffused with passion. "Buddy..."

Then Buddy seemed to mock her.

It was crazy, Amanda knew, looking back, but Buddy seemed to look at her with a vacant, rejecting stare, as if to say, "Can't you do anything right? I'm a friend, just a friend. Clean me up and let me get some rest."

Amanda rubbed Buddy's back and shoulders, hoping to relax the taut figure. No response, just mute, rejecting silence.

"Go fuck yourself!" Amanda had yelled, unable to control herself.

Buddy seemed to sneer. *To sneer!*

Admittedly, Buddy came with a manufacturing defect that gave the lines forming his mouth a slightly irregular downward cast, which looked like a frown or a sneer. A bit like Elvis's famous sneer, actually. Buddy's sneer, if it was a sneer, was accentuated by the dusky light in the cell that fateful night. It spelled rejection in letters too big for Amanda to ignore.

And so Amanda wondered, not for the first time, was she a loser, even in this ersatz love on which she'd hoped to live out her prison days? When you came right down to it, could Buddy be interested, really interested, in a lonely, pathetic convict like her? Even her name, Amanda, seemed girly and a little pathetic, more fitting for a cheerleader than a self-respecting felon.

And where did one go when a relationship with a Cell Buddy went south? I mean, how embarrassing is that? It's not like you can drag your little friend to counseling and expect to hold your head up on the tier or in the prison yard. "Hi, my name is Amanda. Buddy and I are in counseling. We hope to work things out." Not happening, not in this woman's prison.

That sneer, if it was a sneer, set Amanda off. She tore the cell apart, she ranted and screamed, she banged her fists on the steel cell door, she cried tears of impotent rage. And then she slammed Buddy into the wall, tearing his plastic skin, letting the air escape and leaving Buddy a broken figure, crumpled in the corner of a cell that looked like a war zone.

"I hate you," Amanda had screamed. "You stupid plastic faggot, you can go to hell for all I care!"

Later, shocked at what she had done, Amanda sought forgiveness. "It'll never happen again, Bud, I swear. Trust me." Even as she spoke, she heard Dan's words in her head. "It'll never happen again, Babe, I swear. Trust me."

Wiping tears from her eyes, Amanda tried to pump Buddy back up. The little body would expand a bit but then the air would escape with a whoosh. Same with the head, which had a separate air chamber that had been damaged. Amanda vowed to fix Buddy and start their relationship fresh. They'd be friends, dear friends, she said to herself, and see where things went from there. "We'll give it a go, Bud. We can make it work."

"We can make it work," Dan would say, until he decided that it worked for him and that was all that mattered.

Amanda knew it would be hard to find the supplies needed to make Buddy right. And Amanda couldn't help but wonder, deep in her heart, whether Buddy would ever trust her. And whether she, Amanda, could ever be there for Buddy, when the chips were down and the desolation of a prison night held them both in its grasp.

"It'll be all right, Bud," Amanda said, as she snuggled up against the now rumpled plastic form that was her Cell Buddy, speaking in a soft, breathy tone, the one she used when she hoped she really meant what she said. "We're in this together."

Together.

Buddy shuddered at the word, or perhaps it was just the way Amanda gripped him tight as she drifted off into a fitful sleep.

Robert Johnson (author) is a professor of justice, law and criminology at American University, and editor & publisher of BleakHouse Publishing. He is a widely published author of fiction and nonfiction dealing with crime and punishment. His short story, "The Practice of Killing," won the Wild Violet Fiction Contest. Johnson's best known work of social science, *Death Work: A Study of the Modern Execution Process*, won the Outstanding Book Award of the Academy of Criminal Justice Sciences.

Rachel Ternes (artist) is an American University honors student majoring in Psychology and a consulting editor for BleakHouse Publishing. Her paintings were published in AU's literary magazine, *AmLit*, in the fall (2011) and spring (2012) issues, being awarded an Honorable Mention in the magazine's fall competition and Best in Show in the spring. Three of her illustrations were published in the 2012 issue of *BleakHouse Review*, one of which earned her a Tacenda Literary Award for Best Artwork.

Cell Buddy is reprinted from JMWW, fall 2007; http://www.jmww.150m.com/Fall07con.html. Adapted for the stage by Ellen W. Kaplan, Chair of Theatre, Smith College (*Tacenda Literary Magazine*, 2011) and read at American University. Cell Buddy also was adapted for the stage by Jordyn Cahill, Gadsden Correctional Facility, in collaboration with Ellen W. Kaplan, and presented under the direction of Ellen W. Kaplan as part of the Kennedy Center's Page to Stage Program, offered under the auspices of the Safe Streets Foundation Prison to Stage Program.

Cell Buddy
A Stage Adaptation

Story by
Robert Johnson

Adapted for the Stage by
Ellen W. Kaplan

Read at American University
April 14, 2011

(The stage is divided into two spaces: inside the cell, and outside the cell. The cell is small, a free-standing wall of bars defines it. In the cell are two bunks - steel cots, one on top of the other. There is also a chair and small table. Outside the cell is a corridor, defined only by lights, and a counter, with a shelf behind.

AMANDA stands at the counter. The COMMISSARY WORKER (an inmate) is behind the counter. On the shelf behind her is a Big Red Box. AMANDA darts glances over her shoulder suspiciously. Self-consciously, she clears her throat. Her voice catches, and she tries again)

AMANDA

Ahhh...one Cell Buddy please.

COMMISSARY WORKER
(bored, barely looking up)

Which model?

AMANDA

Which...what? What do you mean, 'which model'?

COMMISSARY WORKER

C'mon, hon, people are waiting.

AMANDA

I don't know which...the standard goddamn model!

COMMISSARY WORKER

Ok, Ok. Just doin' my job. Black or white?

AMANDA

Huh?

COMMISSARY WORKER

You want black or white? We're out of the mixed race buddies.

AMANDA

They make mixed race Cell Buddies?

COMMISSARY WORKER

We sell all races. This is equal opportunity stuff. Suh-ply and Dee-man - In de Can!

AMANDA
(embarrassed)

A*ll right.*

COMMISSARY WORKER

Been a run on brown. So, which is it, black or...

AMANDA

White! For chrissakes, white!

COMMISSARY WORKER

Papers?

AMANDA

Papers?

COMMISSARY WORKER

They come with papers. Adoption papers. (AMANDA stares; WORKER snaps her fingers) Fill in de Name, Pop it in de Frame.

AMANDA

What frame?

COMMISSARY WORKER

You're supposed to frame the papers. It's a respect thing. Sign here.

> (SHE hands AMANDA the big red box. On the back of the box, we now see, it says "CB-WHITE" in bold letters. AMANDA signs for it and walks into her CELL
>
> AMANDA puts the box on the lower bed in her cell. She opens it, and we see the head and upper torso of the actress playing CELL BUDDY, now in its deflated position; the lower half of the actress's body will stay hidden within the bed. CELL BUDDY is inanimate, though at times s/he comes to life in AMANDA'S imagination. When

20

moving or speaking, BUDDY is slow and
mechanical.

S/he is an object, not a person. Not *quite* a
person.)

                    AMANDA
                (opening box)
Let's kind of keep this to ourselves, a'ight? Not that I care what
they all think....but that commissary gal put me on edge. Whole
thing seems kinda sketchy....What's this here? A pump. How do
you like that? Two-part pump. Al-*right*, here goes.

                                (As she pumps, BUDDY inflates
                                into a full upper-body figure.)

Not bad. You can move some, huh? (At AMANDA'S touch,
BUDDY moves arms, swivels head) You know, some crazy
psychiatrist figured this out – what'd she say? Even convicts need
love...

                    BUDDY
                (as Psychiatrist)
Prison is a lonely place.

                    AMANDA
No kidding. Especially if you're female. Hey, your arms move!

                    BUDDY
                (as Psychiatrist)
The arms are expressly made long, to wrap around the prisoner's
body in a secure embrace.

                                (BUDDY holds out his arms in an embrace.
                                AMANDA backs away – she's not ready for this)

                    AMANDA
                (looks nervously out cell door)
Warden thinks it's a big joke. Easy for her to laugh.

                    BUDDY
                (as Psychiatrist)

Cell Buddies are smooth all over. (Demonstrates by holding up arms) No orifices. No appendages.

AMANDA

We only craving sex, right? Forget *love*. That's what they think!

BUDDY
(as Psychiatrist)

Your Cell Buddy will listen to you. Your Cell Buddy will make your cell a home.

AMANDA
(staring at BUDDY)

Yeah, well. Maybe. (To herself) Some of the worst things that happen to a woman in prison…happen in her cell.

>(DAN, aka Danielle, comes into the cell, slipping in from upstage, not from the actual door of the cell. This is DAN's ghost).

AMANDA
(to BUDDY)

You believe it? There's no men here, but we still got wife-beating.

DAN
(on top bunk, stretching out)

Amanda, babe. Didn't I always tell you. When I'm gone, you get yourself a nice Cell Buddy. Hey, Why be Lonely – Get Yourself a Rubber Homie?

>(AMANDA sits on lower bunk, next to BUDDY. DAN talks as if to himself. AMANDA doesn't want to hear DAN, but deep within, she hears every word.)

DAN

We were good for each other, weren't we, babe? I made you feel *safe*. Dan the Man, your very own butch cellmate. Like having a big tough older brother to protect you.

AMANDA

You made me feel secure. For a while.

DAN

Yeah, well. Safety's an illusion, babe. Specially in prison.

AMANDA

You were a smooth operator.

DAN

I was patient.

AMANDA

I was easy pickings. I was *prey*.

DAN

...for all the other tough butch cons. You couldn't have survived without me.

AMANDA

I trusted you. You said...

DAN

It's either me, babe, or everybody else.

AMANDA

I shoulda seen it coming.

(DAN gets down from the upper bunk, stretches out on Amanda's bunk. AMANDA moves BUDDY to the chair.

DAN

Hey, tidy up my bed, would ya?

AMANDA
(as she makes the upper bed)
But the whole process was slow, subtle.

DAN

Give me a back rub, would ya, babe? (SHE does) Oh, that feels good, just like that.

AMANDA

At first you took it slow, subtle like. Ask for little things I would have done anyway.

DAN

Warm up my coffee.

AMANDA

Then you gave orders. Like some perverted kind of King or
something, like in the Bible.

DAN
(tougher now)

I want my bed made, my laundry done, my food served hot while I
lay naked here in bed.

AMANDA

And sex of course.

DAN

On *my* terms.

AMANDA

On *your* terms. But mostly, you wanted me to be your slave.

DAN

You're a piece of meat, babe. (stands, grabs AMANDA, throws her
against the bed) My punching bag. (he hits her, she goes down on
the bed, screams) But only on my bad days.

AMANDA
(she sits up, rubs her head)

(to BUDDY) There are a lot of bad days in prison.

DAN

You *are* my slave. Don't forget it. (he lies back on the lower bunk).

AMANDA

And I didn't.

DAN

Rub my feet.

AMANDA
(she does)

I was meek, docile.

DAN

That's good. Helps me sleep.

AMANDA

Sure, Dan. Whatever you say.

> (DAN yawns, turns over on his stomach, sleeping
> deeply)

AMANDA
(pulls out a homemade knife)

He never saw it coming. (AMANDA plunges knife into DAN's
back. DAN screams. She covers his face with a pillow, then pulls
out the knife. AMANDA speaks to BUDDY) I did it. I plunged it
into his back while he slept. I made it, hid it, used it. This shiv saved
my life.

DAN
(stands up, straightens his clothes)

It's a *shank*, Amanda. Not a shiv. Callin' it a shiv, that's gay. You
put a *shank* into me. Killed me, you did. Now you're all alone.

> (DAN strolls out of cell and off. SOUND: prison at night.
> Low voices; muffled screams, cries.)

AMANDA
(to BUDDY)

Prison at night is a scary place. You listen to the cries, and they tell
you the thing you never want to hear, that the world is cold and hard
and you are completely alone. (hugs BUDDY) Buddy. (AMANDA
leads BUDDY to her bed, talks to him, touches him gently) Buddy.
Stay with me, while I sleep….(she drifts off to sleep)

BUDDY
(softly speaks)

Could make stone speak of life's hard ends
With words that shine like darkling Gems
I was here
I am a woman
I bleed, therefore I am

25

AMANDA

Don't stop, Buddy.

BUDDY

Alive, in a manner of speaking
It's raw, sweet freedom I'm desperately seeking
A prison cell's a coffin reeking
Of dreams gone sour
Of life died by the hour
Of death by decree
Until you're set free
In this life or the next.[1]

        (AMANDA wakes, takes BUDDY'S hand, looks
        into his eyes)

AMANDA

Good morning, Buddy. (she gets up, starts to pump air out of
BUDDY – the actress 'collapses' again) I'm gonna let the air out of
you, cause today you're coming out on the block with me. Let 'em
laugh. Half of them have their own buddies. Just tuck you under my
arm. "You mess with Buddy, you come up bloody!"

        (AMANDA goes to commissary window. She has
        a shirt that is exactly the same as the one BUDDY
        is wearing. She carries the shirt carefully,
        tenderly, as if it were BUDDY himself. The 'real'
        BUDDY is collapsed on AMANDA's bed.)

AMANDA

        (muttering, to unseen inmates)
Yeah, I know what you're thinking. Boy toy. You got yours, hidden
in plain sight, what's that tucked into your shirt, puffing it out like
it's some kind of shank-proof vest. I don't give a shit.

COMMISSARY WORKER

No mail.

---

[1] Lines drawn from the poem, "Desperately Seeking Freedom," by
Robert Johnson. *A Zoo Near You*, BleakHouse Publishing,
2010:116.

AMANDA

What d'ya mean, no mail?

COMMISSARY WORKER

Like I said, you got *no mail*.

AMANDA

Shit! (she storms away) Shit. Haven't gotten a fucking letter in ages...Hey, watch it! What the fuck are you doing?

> (SHE stumbles, as if someone has bumped into her. 'BUDDY' – the shirt – falls to the ground. AMANDA picks it up, furious)

You old bitch! What you falling on me like you can't stand on your two goddamed feet! You got grease and shit all over him, the floor's freaking filthy. Get out of my face, you fuckin old witch.

> (SHE runs back to her cell, where she pumps up the 'real' BUDDY. Still agitated. As she begins to calm down, she starts stroking BUDDY. Slowly, rhythmically, gently, she begins to make love to BUDDY. She lies BUDDY on his back, climbs on top, stares into his eyes, passion growing.)

AMANDA

Buddy...Buddy...

BUDDY

(sits up, sneers)

Can't you do anything right? I'm a friend. Just a friend. Clean me up and let me get some rest.

AMANDA

(jumping up like she's been stung)

What the...Go fuck yourself!

BUDDY

You think I could really be excited by some lonely pathetic convict like you?

27

AMANDA
(enraged, screaming)
Shut up! I hate you! (during this, AMANDA tears the cell apart,
bangs and throws everything, slams BUDDY against the wall, then
punches him the way DAN had punched her) You stupid plastic
faggot, you can go to hell for all I care!

(BUDDY collapses on the floor. AMANDA
stares, horrified)

AMANDA
(goes to him, tries to pick him up)
It'll never happen again, Bud, I swear. Trust me.

(DAN appears on the top bed)

DAN
It'll never happen again, Babe. Trust me.

AMANDA
(starts to cry)
I'll fix it. We'll start over. (she attempts to pump up BUDDY, as at
the beginning. BUDDY keeps collapsing over) We'll be friends.
Dear friends. We'll give it a go, Bud. We'll make it work.

DAN
(from above)
We'll make it work. (PAUSE) It worked for me.

AMANDA
(puts BUDDY on bed, snuggles up)
It'll be alright, Bud. We're in this together.

(BUDDY shudders. AMANDA drifts off to a
fitful sleep)

Robert Johnson (author) is a professor of justice, law and criminology at American University, and editor & publisher of BleakHouse Publishing. He is a widely published author of fiction and nonfiction dealing with crime and punishment. His short story, "The Practice of Killing," won the Wild Violet Fiction Contest. Johnson's best known work of social science, *Death Work: A Study of the Modern*

Execution Process, won the Outstanding Book Award of the Academy of Criminal Justice Sciences.

Ellen W. Kaplan (playwright & director) is Chair of Theatre, former Director of Jewish Studies, and Professor of Acting and Directing at Smith College, and a three-time Fulbright Scholar/Senior Scholar. She is an actor, director and playwright; she has taught and directed across the U.S., in Costa Rica (in Spanish), Israel, and most recently, in Shenyang, China; her plays have won awards and been presented internationally. She has published a book, *Images of Mental Illness in Text and Performance*, as well as poetry, prose and scholarly essays. Ellen is also active in theatre outreach; recent projects include theatre work with incarcerated mothers and adjudicated teens, as well as teaching a course based on the Inside-Out Training Program for teaching in prisons.

Rachel Ternes (artist) is an American University honors student majoring in Psychology and a consulting editor for BleakHouse Publishing. Her paintings were published in AU's literary magazine, *AmLit*, in the fall (2011) and spring (2012) issues, being awarded an Honorable Mention in the magazine's fall competition and Best in Show in the spring. Three of her illustrations were published in the 2012 issue of *BleakHouse Review*, one of which earned her a Tacenda Literary Award for Best Artwork.

Cell Buddy
A Stage Adaptation

Story by
Robert Johnson

Adapted for the Stage by
Jordyn Cahill
&
Ellen W. Kaplan

Directed by
Ellen W. Kaplan
Read at the Kennedy Center
September 1, 2012

Characters

Amanda: A younger white girl in prison who is now serving a life sentence for the murder of her lover, Dan-the-Man, a former female inmate. Amanda has slowly become mentally unstable and erratic due to the physical, emotional and mental abuse and trauma sustained at the hands of Dan. She has a "relationship" with a blow-up doll named Buddy.

Flaca: An Hispanic-American inmate housed on the tier with Amanda who acts as antagonist to Amanda. Flaca is very dramatic and very "Latina" in her speech and behaviors.

Lisa: A new inmate to the tier who is being told the story of Amanda's circumstances and the relationship she has with her blow-up doll, Buddy. Lisa is sarcastic and witty, but unaware of the prison system, so she is very inquisitive.

Dan-the-Man: A white, masculine woman in prison who is the epitome of a prison "thug". Dan is played as a flashback whenever he appears, along with Flashback Amanda. Dan is very controlling and very manipulative as well. Dan is physically larger than Amanda and very domineering in presence.

Flashback Amanda: This character is a physical replica of Amanda.

Scene set-up

There is a metal picnic table set up at the front, down-stage right portion of the stage. A large cell without bars is located down-stage left to give the audience full view of Amanda, who will be contained within the cell the duration of the play. Flaca and Lisa will be seated at the table holding the conversation.

Opening scene

(*Lights come up* on Amanda's cell as she sits on her bed, as Buddy is strapped to a chair by his overly long arms, a strip of cloth tied around his mouth. Flaca and Lisa are seated, watching the entire exchange and sniggering.)

33

Amanda: (singing) "My Buddy, My Buddy. Wherever I go you go too. My Buddy. My Buddy." Now, if you think that you can behave, I will un-tie you. However, if you so much as sneer at me, your punishment will be swift and severe. Okay, Budster?

> (*Amanda unties* Buddy's hands and takes the cloth from around his head. Amanda then goes into her foot locker.)

Now, today for lunch, we are having peanut butter on tortillas and lemonade. (Turning to Buddy) Excuse me? Well, if you don't like it, don't eat it. In fact, I think you're getting a bit lippy again Mr. Mister.

> (*Picks up* the cloth and dangles it in front of Buddy's face)

You are making me do this. I have asked you nice-as-pie too many times now to just be grateful. But, no, you sit there all high and mighty and look at me like I am crazy. (Raising her voice) I am not crazy and I refuse to be treated as though I am....!

Flaca: Hey, Looney-Tunes, I don' think that friggin' doll can hear you, okay? Else he'd be tunin' you out coz he don't like that way you speaks to him.

Amanda: Listen Mexico, I don't tell you how to do handle your lady ----don't tell me how to handle mine, 'kay?

Flaca: Firs' off, I ain't Mexican, I'm Puerto Rican, gringo. Second this ain't my lady, this is the new girl on D-4 and Sarge tol' me to show her around and since you the biggest looney around here I figgered I'd show her you. So, you wanna introduce yourself, be my gues', or I can tell her who jou is.

Amanda: My name is Amanda Lattimore and I have been here for 8 years. I came in with 2 years and now I have life. How's that Cuban?

Flaca: It's Puerto Rican, jackass.

Lisa: How did you come in with 2 years and now you have life? Can they just do that to people?

Flaca: They can if you kill your stud girlfriend while she sleeps.

Lisa: You killed your girlfriend?

Amanda: Yup, Dan the Man.

Lisa: Dan is a man's name.

Flaca: Honey, round here, things ain't always what they seem. Like, you'll be walking track and look over and you think you see Tom Cruise and then you get a little closer and Tom's got him a set of c-cups, cuz Tom is actually Tamara. That's how Dan was before Spice Girl over here did her...him in.

Amanda: Fidel here acts like she don' know how it is. Ask her about "Jay-Z."

Lisa: You mean the rapper?

Flaca: Jay-Z is a chick, but that what she goes by in here. Lots of girls do that. They come in and uh get all beefed up. Before you know it, Shaquanda's Shaggy and Jameisha's Jay-Z. You might like one yourself.

Lisa: Yeah, I don't think that's gonna happen. So how did you do it? If it's okay that I ask?

Flaca: Loca don't mind. We gonna be the only people she'll talk to today except Half-Man tied to the chair in there.

Amanda: Thank you asshole, but as you see, I have untied him and so long as he remains good, he will remain that way. Well, when I first got here, I was scared. I had never been locked up before and the place scared the shit out of me. I looked a lot like you. Naïve. People were starting to take it for weakness. Dan was nice. He was really good about not letting anyone fuck with me. He had a lot of respect here and when I was out with him, people showed me respect, too. He was like a brother at first, albeit one with boobs.

Flaca: Yeah, thas' jus' like, "This mister is my sister, yo."

Lisa: (grabbing at the crotch of her pants) "Yeah, they call me Rico. One of you ho's gotta tampon?" (All three women laugh)

Amanda: That's exactly how Dan was. One minute she would be all "mannish" and the next she'd be whining and crying like a little girl. Dan, or Danielle as her mother named her, was girlier than me before she came here. I snooped in her locker once and found pictures of her in a bikini and… with a man.

Flaca: Bullshit…you mean Dan likes boys?

Lisa: So, how did you two…?

Amanda: I was friggin lonely, that's how. This place is scary as hell at night. You can almost feel the ghosts of all the women who've lived here before. Sometimes, you can even hear them.

Flaca: Nah, man. You can't hear no shit like that. That's only the voices in her freakin' head and shit. The most you hear is like bed squeaks and cryin'. I ain't never heard no damn voices. That's crazy people shit.

Amanda: Can you believe this chick, babe? (Circling her finger and mouthing "crazy") Anyway, he was real cool and always looked out for me. He started asking me things like, "Hey, babe, can you make me a cup of coffee when I get back in from work, so I don't have to fight for the microwave after count clears?" or, "Amanda, my shoulders are killing me, can you give me a little massage. It wasn't like caveman shit. "You woman, my woman. Food, sex, now." That bastard was smooth like Oil of Olay and as sweet as sugar.

> (*Lights down* on Amanda's cell and the common-area. Lights up on stage right. There are two beds set perpendicular to one another to recreate the typical holding cell. Dan and Flashback Amanda are seated on the bed and Amanda is crying. Dan is being sympathetic.)

Dan: You knew it was gonna happen eventually. No man sticks around.

Flashback Amanda: But he promised. He knew I didn't have anyone else. He was it. We were going to…get married. (Sobs)

Dan: (Rubs her back and strokes her hair) Ah, now don't cry. That son of a bitch don't know what he's missin'. Amanda, you are beautiful, smart, funny...

Flashback Amanda: No I'm not. If I was, he'd still be here! He never would have left. I wouldn't be alone right now.

Dan: You aren't alone. I'm here. Okay.

Flashback Amanda: But ...that's different.

Dan: It doesn't have to be. You can pretend I'm your man.

Flashback Amanda: (trying to be funny) But, Dan, you're a girl.

Dan: No, it's a lie I say! For real?

Flashback Amanda: (playfully hitting Dan) Stop. You know what I mean. You know I'm not...uhm...

Dan: Gay?

Flashback Amanda: Yeah, I've never done...that.

Dan: It'll just be pretend, like playin' house. I bring home the bacon and you cook it up or whatever.

Flashback Amanda: Promise?

Dan: Yeah, I promise. Now make my food bitch!

Flashback Amanda: Dan! (Laughs and playfully smacks Dan; *cross fade* to Amanda's cell and common area table.)

Amanda: It wasn't serious at first. I was only like playing house. Dan was my friend and we happened to live together, kind of like my relationship with Buddy.

Flaca: Here we go with the looney-shit again

Amanda: Taco Bell, I advise you to keep your mouth shut when I speak about my relationships.

Flaca: (zipping her mouth) Not another word.

Amanda: Dan was really cool at first. He'd come in from work and I'd have his clothes laid out, a cup of coffee and food. Everything was fine until that one day. I shouldn't have gone to rec. I should have just stayed in. none of this would have happened.

(*Cross fade*) (Cell Amanda enters stage right.)

Flashback Amanda: (Calling out over her shoulder) See you tomorrow. Bye...

Dan: (Grabbing and swinging her around) Where in the fuck you been?

Flashback Amanda: A...at...rec...why? What happened?

Dan: I got off early that's what! How in the fuck can you just be hanging out when I'm at work all day?

Flashback Amanda: I was only gone an hour. You weren't supposed to be back til...

Dan: (shaking her) Don't tell me when I'm supposed to be home. You are supposed to have my shit cleaned and this place cleaned up. From the looks of things, you ain't keeping up your end of the bargain.

Flashback Amanda: Dan, I'm sorry. I...just...I'm on the volleyball team and we had practice. I'll...

Dan: (Slaps Amanda across the face) The fucking volleyball team? Who told you you was allowed to get on the volleyball team? You ain't gonna be wearin' those little shorts with all them studs around and make a fool of me.

Flashback Amanda: Dan, I didn't think this was...

Dan: What, a relationship? You didn't think what, Amanda? So far as I remember, I take care of you and we live together. That seems like a relationship to me.

Flashback Amanda: But you're the one who said it was like…only pretend.

Dan: Bullshit. You're not stupid and neither am I. in fact, I think it's about time shit startin' changing around here. We are in a relationship and you are gonna act like a wife should.

Flashback Amanda: What…does that mean, Dan?

Dan: You know exactly what the fuck I mean. You better get your shit together. I'm going to take a shower and I'm hungry so, have me something to eat when I get out.

Flashback Amanda: Okay, Dan. I'm sorry.

Dan: And?

Flashback Amanda: And I promise to do better.

Dan: That's what I thought.

(*Leans in* to kiss Amanda, she flinches. Dan laughs.)

Don't worry baby, you'll get used to it.

(*Cross fade* to cell)

Lisa: So, why did you go along with it?

Flaca: It ain't that easy around here. You say something to the POPO and the next thing you know you bof go to jail, then they investigate and say it's your word against hers, and now you nothin' but a snitch.

Lisa: So, you just kept on?

Amanda: Pretty much. Dan would go to work and I would clean, do the laundry, make the food, give her massages, write nasty sex letters so she could get money, and any other thing she wanted me to do. I didn't have anyone else. It was a matter of survival. Plus, I loved her. I know she loved me too.

Lisa: Sounds like Stockholm Syndrome to me.

Flaca: Ooh, I had that once. It burned soooo bad.. (Amanda and Lisa look at Flaca) What?

Amanda: It figures you'd think it was VD.

Lisa: It's a mental thing where people end up being sympathetic to the people keeping them hostage. Like, you learn to depend on them because they are all you have and because of that , you see them as your hero or something. I read it in a book.

Amanda: Dan wasn't always mean. Sometimes he was really good to me and he did take care of me...but something always brought his asshole side out and I was the punching bag.

> (*Cross fade* to Cell. Amanda enters stage right and opens a letter. Dan is seated on a bed with the radio on.)

Flashback Amanda: Oh my God. He wrote. (Opens the letter, reads)

Dan: (Nonchalantly) Who? Who wrote you?

Flashback Amanda: Paul did...after all this time. I can't believe it.

Dan: So, what the hell does that mean? I thought you didn't care what he thought? I thought you didn't think about him? Answer me!

Flashback Amanda: (crying) I...I...I...don't know wh...what to say, Dan. We had a life together. How can you expect me to just forget him?

Dan: Don't do that pity party shit with me Amanda. You know damn well how I feel about this. You ain't writin' his ass back.

Flashback Amanda: I don't say anything about you writing Alicia do I? No I don't.

Dan: That's different.

Flashback Amanda: How is it different? You lived together and you had sex and you both said you loved each other and...

Dan: (lunges forward and grabs Amanda by the throat) Don't talk to me like that. Do not think you can threaten me. You think you know me, but you don't. You don't know what I will do to you if you cross me. Do you understand me? Do you fucking understand me, Amanda?

(*Cross fade*)

Amanda: (holding Buddy by the throat) You rotten bitch! You will not disrespect me! I take care of you and all you do is take me for granted. You are ungrateful and good for nothing. What? You can't breathe? Oh, poor baby, can't breathe...

Dan: You don't get it bitch! You need you a little lesson.

(*Dan throws* Flashback Amanda to the ground and as lights fade, she screams. As Dan hits Flashback Amanda, Amanda screams)

Amanda: (Throws Buddy to the bed and screams along with Flashback Amanda as Dan hits her) Ahhhhhh! Stop!

Dan: (Hitting her) I'll kill you!!

(*Cross fade*)

Amanda: (cries) It was worse. She was the only person I had and the only one I could trust. She hurt me, but I trusted her. She told me this place would eat me alive and she was right. Only, it was her.

Lisa: (To Flaca) Did you know about this?

Flaca: Yeah, but you don't say nothin'. If it ain't your bizness, you keep your mouth shut,

Lisa: (Obviously bothered) See, I don't buy that. That's like saying the kid next door's getting beat to death and you just shut the damn blinds and turn away and that's bullshit.

Flaca: Yeah, but in here, thas' jus' the way it is. It's either that, or you get beat down. These people ain't nice. They ain't here for selling cookies, yo. Look at her. She offed Dan for real.

Lisa: How did you do it?

Amanda: I just did it.

> (*As Amanda speaks* in her cell, she narrates what is happening in the flashback cell. Dim lights come up on Flashback Amanda and Dan's cell. Beast of Burden from the Rolling Stones is playing softly in the background. Dan is sleeping on her stomach and Flashback Amanda is sitting at the edge of her bed crying softly. She stands up on her bed and reaches up into a light fixture and grabs her shank. As she steps down onto the floor, she looks down, raises the shank above her head with both hands and drives it into Dan's back. Dan screams once and goes limp. Flashback Amanda lies down on her bed, covers up and rolls over to go to sleep.)

Amanda: She was asleep. She had beaten me pretty badly for not washing her clothes out right. My eye was swollen and my head was killing me. Had the shank for protection, but she never knew. It just hit me, she wasn't going to stop and I wasn't strong enough to stop her. It was like I was watching myself from above, like it wasn't really me. I climbed up on my bed and grabbed it from the light fixture. I can remember when I climbed down, I prayed silently for God to help me. I raised my hands above my head and...I just stuck it into her back again and again and again. She screamed once and then went limp. I got back into my bed, rolled over, and went to sleep.

> (*Cross fade*)

Amanda: Sergeant Barrett came and got me the next morning. One of the girls next to us woke up that morning and saw Dan covered in blood. The shank was on the floor. I was too numb to care what they did to me. It wouldn't matter anyway, right?

Lisa: But it does matter. She was abusive.

Amanda: I wasn't in the middle of being beaten. They don't care around here how things are. They only care how things look. Instead of getting out in two years, I've got a life sentence to complete. Me and Buddy. He's gonna do it right along with me.

(*Amanda picks up* Buddy and holds him tightly.)

Flaca: (imitating Tony Montana from Scarface) Say hello to my little friend. (Amanda glares at Flaca and she puts her hands up defensively) Jus' jokin' man. Don' be so serious okay.

Lisa: So, how did, um, you and Buddy…meet?

Amanda: Buddy was a 'ho and selling himself at the canteen.

Lisa: What?

Amanda: (laughing) A while back this shrink decides it was beneficial for us "lonely" inmates that we have companionship, even if it was the rubber kind. He said just to be in the room with someone else, we would be less likely to suffer from depression. So, DOC started selling Buddies on the canteen and I bought him.

Flaca: They sol' black ones and Espanol ones, I even saw a East Indian one, man. Chick took a dress and made a turban and took a sharpie and made one of them little forehead dots.

(*pointing* to Amanda)

She don' believe in race mixin' so she stuck with a good ol' white boy. I'm surprised she didn' name him Bubba like a redneck.

Amanda: Better to be a redneck than a wetback. Buddy and I were just friends at first. But after they put me in solitary for Dan. I didn't have anyone to talk to. They let us out for an hour a day and we could go to the store on the quad and I waited until everyone had gone out to rec and went and got him.

Flaca: Finally, the truth comes out.

Lisa: So, does it help?

Amanda: Buddy and I have a very deep relationship. (Puts her nose to his) Don't we, honey?

(Lisa and Flaca look at each other, amused)

Amanda: Look at it this way. I don't have to bother with any of those bitches out there if I have him. He is always there and even when he's being stubborn he listens to me and we fight and make up.

Flaca: Like, uh, make-up make-up, if you know what I mean?

Lisa: I just can't see myself shacked up with a doll. Sorry. I mean if it works for you, great. It's just not for me. I can handle being lonely. I've been lonely a long time so doing it in here is a cake-walk. No chicks and no dolls.

Amanda: We'll see. Buddy and I are in this thing together now. There is no more "me" or "I", it's us from here on out. There have been times when I thought I was losing it for sure...

Flaca: Ain't no freakin' shocker there, huh, homes?

Amanda: At first, things were really great. (Clutches Buddy to her chest, rocking back and forth) "O'er the cell a mark still lingers, of where a convict's bloodied fingers could make stone speak of life's hard ends with words that shine like darkling gems. I was here. I am woman. I bleed therefore I am, alive in a manner of speaking. It's raw, sweet freedom I'm desperately seeking. A prison cell's a coffin reeking of dreams gone sour, of life died by the hour, of death by decree, until you're set free in this life or the next."

This place is like a tomb. I'm trapped now. I would have been home last year if not for....

We talk. But it isn't always cozy. Like any relationship. We argue and disagree, too. We fight just like other couples do.

Lisa: Does Buddy hit you?

Flaca: Are you freakin' kiddin' me?

Amanda: No.

Lisa: (Suspiciously) Do you hit Buddy?

Amanda: Wh…what? Why would you ask me that? Of course not. I love Buddy.

Lisa: What's the duct tape on his arms and necks for?

Amanda: He…uh…popped a couple of times and I had to try and, uh, fix him…

> (*Lights go down* on Amanda and the common area table. Lights come up on Buddy and Amanda's cell. Buddy is propped up on a pillow against the wall and Amanda is pacing the cell. As she paces she hits her hands into her hands and is yelling more than talking)

Amanda: What do you mean you don't know? Answer me, damnit! I asked you if you thought she was cute and you only nodded. What is that supposed to mean?

> (*Pulling* at her hair)

Buddy, I do so much for you and you are so damn inconsiderate. You have no idea how damn good you have it. I have gone out of my way for your rubber ass since the first day I got you. I have only loved you. It is clear now that you don't give a fuck about me and that maybe if you saw the other side, you would appreciate me more. (Holds her hand out as thought Buddy is interrupting her.) No, you cannot explain, you have had your chances. Don't fucking sneer at me! I have told you…(screaming) shut up! Shut up! Shut up!

> (*Amanda lunges* and begins to choke Buddy)

I hate you, you stupid plastic faggot! You can go to hell for all I care!

> (*Amanda slams* buddy into the walls and he pops loudly.)

Amanda: I don't know. Not too many people can understand Buddy and my relationship, I don't feel really comfortable just talking to anyone. Maybe I can just talk to you guys.

Flaca: (skeptically) What, like friends?

Amanda: I don't know. Maybe.

Lisa: Hey, I don't mind. I need to get back to my altruistic side anyway.

Flaca: Is that like where your mother's like Haitian or somethin'?

Lisa: No, it's just doing something for others just to be good.

Flaca: Oh, okay. Yeah man, I can be altruistic, too.

> (*Recall* for count-time is announced over the P.A. system)

Lisa: Look, I'm only right down there, so if you need to talk to me, just holler.

Flaca: Oh God, white girl jus' said holler. Nex' thing you know, they'll be roastin' a pig in a pit and doin' keg stands.

Amanda: Hey, Flaca? Don't you have to pack out?

Flaca: Pack out? For what?

Amanda: 'Cause I thought I just saw INS pulling up.

Flaca: You are so berry freakin' funny. Adios, loca.

Amanda: Right back at ya, Burrito.

> (*Amanda sits* Buddy up on the bed and sits on the bed opposite him, facing the audience.)

Amanda: Listen Buddy, we've got to talk. I've been doing a lot of thinking and I really think we should take some time off. It's for the best, Buddy. I just really feel like we've both been hurt a lot and we need to focus on getting better. I still want to be friends and maybe we can hang out now and then, but I feel like right now it's just best that we say our goodbyes.

(*Amanda holds* her hand up to stop Buddy from interrupting)

Don't beg. I can't handle when you beg me. I have to steel myself and my resolve. I've made my decision and it's final. What? One last hug? Okay. I think that's fair. All right, come here little fella.

(*Amanda picks* up Buddy as lights fade and lights go down.)

(There is a loud pop)

Amanda: I told you it was over.

Robert Johnson (author) is a professor of justice, law and criminology at American University, and editor & publisher of BleakHouse Publishing. He is a widely published author of fiction and nonfiction dealing with crime and punishment. His short story, "The Practice of Killing," won the Wild Violet Fiction Contest. Johnson's best known work of social science, *Death Work: A Study of the Modern Execution Process*, won the Outstanding Book Award of the Academy of Criminal Justice Sciences.

Jordyn Cahill (playwright) is a Gadsden Correctional Facility inmate nearing the end of her sentence. While confined, she wrote several original stories, one of which, "Frozen," appears in the 2012 issue of *Tacenda Literary Magazine*. Cahill is author of the stage adaptation of Gumbo, presented at the Kennedy Center in 2011.

Ellen W. Kaplan (playwright & director) is Chair of Theatre, former Director of Jewish Studies, and Professor of Acting and Directing at Smith College, and a three-time Fulbright Scholar/Senior Scholar. She is an actor, director and playwright; she has taught and directed across the U.S., in Costa Rica (in Spanish), Israel, and most recently, in Shenyang, China; her plays have won awards and been presented internationally. She has published a book, *Images of Mental Illness in Text and Performance*, as well as poetry, prose and scholarly essays. Ellen is also active in theatre outreach; recent projects include theatre work with incarcerated mothers and adjudicated teens, as well as teaching a course based on the Inside-Out Training Program for teaching in prisons.

Rachel Ternes (artist) is an American University honors student majoring in Psychology and a consulting editor for BleakHouse Publishing. Her paintings were published in AU's literary magazine, *AmLit*, in the fall (2011) and spring (2012) issues, being awarded an Honorable Mention in the magazine's fall competition and Best in Show in the spring. Three of her illustrations were published in the 2012 issue of *BleakHouse Review*, one of which earned her a Tacenda Literary Award for Best Artwork.